The WiFi Networking Book
WLAN Standards: IEEE 802.11 bgn, 802.11n, 802.11ac and 802.11ax

Gordon Colbach

gordon.colbach@cloudversity.com

ISBN-13: 9781073328420

REVISION 4

This book is updated regularly and will expand and elaborate on the topic over time. The updates are tracked through a revision number noted above. Updates log can be found in the pages ahead.

If you have already bought an ebook or hard copy then we would be happy to provide you the free ebook of the latest version. Please send an email to the author at gordon.colbach@cloudversity.com to claim your free copy.

CONTENTS

UPDATES

If you have any feedback regarding this book, any errata that you wish to report or updates that you wish to see please shoot out an email to gordon.colbach@cloudversity.com .

As a token of appreciation we will send out an Amazon gift card for every suggestion that we receive.

Update Log

1. 16 Jun 2019 - Launch

2. 20 Sep 2019 - Illustrations added. Grammar fixes.

3. 25 Sep 2019 - Content update.

4. 09 Oct 2019 - Content update. Future Amendments to 802.11

1. INTRODUCTION

A wireless network is a flexible data communications system, which uses wireless media such as radio frequency technology to transmit and receive data over the air, minimizing the need for wired connections. Wireless networks are used to augment rather than replace wired networks and are most commonly used to provide last few stages of connectivity between a mobile user and a wired network.

Wireless networks use electromagnetic waves to communicate information from one point to another without relying on any physical connection. Radio waves are often referred to as radio carriers because they simply perform the function of delivering energy to a remote receiver.

The data being transmitted is superimposed on the radio carrier so that it can be accurately extracted at the receiving end. Once data is superimposed (modulated) onto the radio carrier, the radio signal occupies more than a single frequency, since the frequency or bit rate of the modulating information adds to the carrier.

Multiple radio carriers can exist in the same space at the same time without interfering with each other if the radio waves are transmitted on different radio frequencies. To extract data, a radio receiver tunes in one radio frequency while rejecting all other frequencies. The modulated signal thus received is then demodulated and the data is extracted from the signal.

Figure: Wireless Technology

Wireless networks offer the following productivity, convenience, and cost advantages over traditional wired networks:

- **Mobility**: provide mobile users with access to real-time information so that they can roam around in the network without getting disconnected from the network. This mobility supports productivity and service opportunities not possible with wired networks.

- **Installation speed and simplicity**: installing a wireless system can be fast and easy and can eliminate the need to pull cable through walls and ceilings.

- **Reach of the network**: the network can be extended to places which can not be wired

11

- **More Flexibility**: wireless networks offer more flexibility and adapt easily to changes in the configuration of the network.

- **Reduced cost of ownership**: while the initial investment required for wireless network hardware can be higher than the cost of wired network hardware, overall installation expenses and life- cycle costs can be significantly lower in dynamic environments.

- **Scalability**: wireless systems can be configured in a variety of topologies to meet the needs of specific applications and installations. Configurations can be easily changed and range from peer-to-peer networks suitable for a small number of users to larger infrastructure networks that enable roaming over a broad area.

2. WIRELESS USAGE SCENARIOS

There are three primary usage scenarios for wireless connectivity [1]:

1. Wireless Personal Area Networking (WPAN)
2. Wireless Local Area Networking (WLAN)
3. Wireless Wide Area Networking (WWAN)

WPAN describes an application of wireless technology that is intended to address usage scenarios that are inherently personal in nature. The emphasis is on instant connectivity between devices that manage personal data or which facilitate data sharing between small groups of individuals.

An example might be synchronizing data between a PDA and a desktop computer. Or another example might be spontaneous sharing of a document between two or more individuals. The nature of these types of data sharing scenarios is that they are ad hoc and often spontaneous. Wireless communication adds value for these types of usage models by reducing complexity (i.e. eliminates the need for cables).

---

[1] "Bluetooth wireless technology basics - HP."
http://www.hp.com/ctg/Manual/c00186949.pdf. Accessed 6 Nov. 2017.

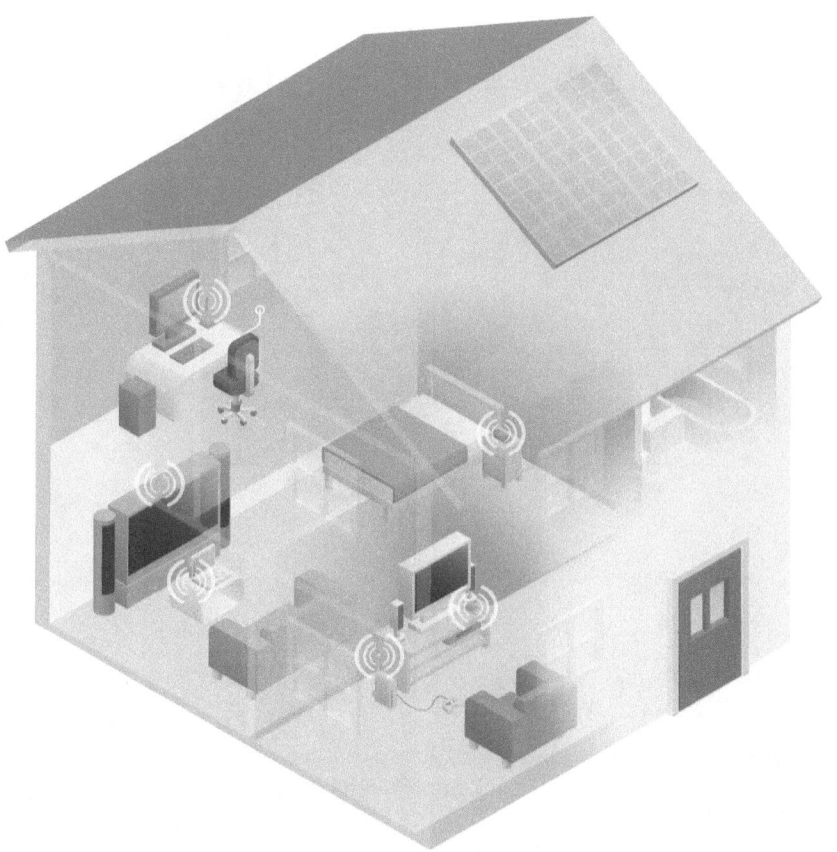

**Figure: A home network uses both WLAN and WPAN
technologies.**

WLAN on the other hand is more focused on organizational
connectivity not unlike wire based LAN connections. The intent of WLAN
technologies is to provide members of workgroups access to corporate
network resources be it shared data, shared applications or e-mail but do so in
a way that does not inhibit a user's mobility. The emphasis is on a permanence
of the wireless connection within a defined region like an office building or
campus. This implies that there are wireless access points that define a finite
region of coverage.

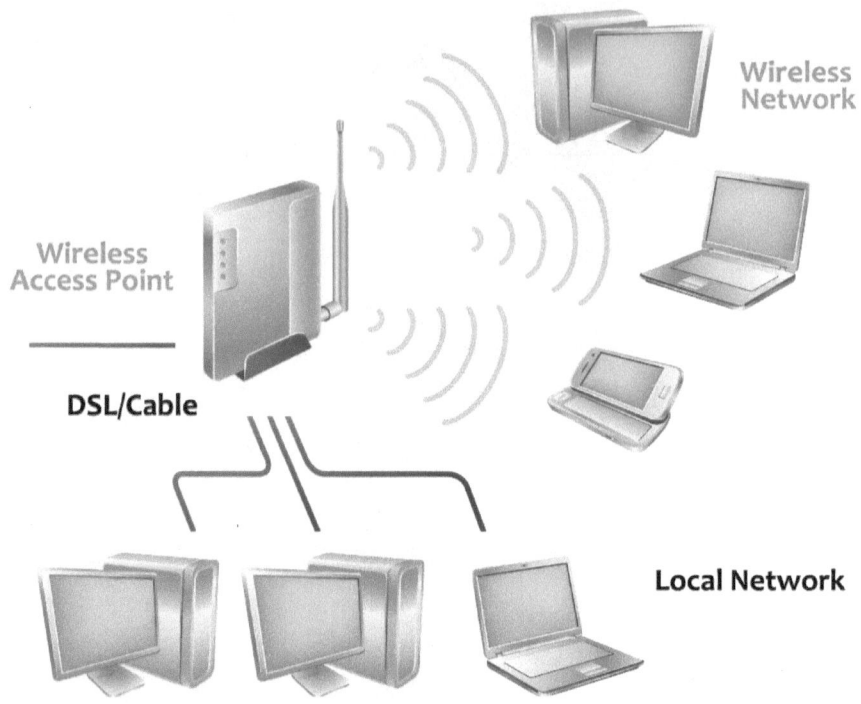

Figure: Wireless Local Area Networks are often extensions of Wired Local Networks

Whereas WLAN addresses connectivity within a defined region, WWAN addresses the need to stay connected while traveling outside this boundary. Today, cellular technologies enable wireless computer connectivity either via a cable to a cellular telephone or through PC Card cellular modems. The need being addressed by WWAN is the need to stay in touch with business critical communications while traveling.

The following table summarizes each wireless connectivity usage scenario by a wireless technology.

Table 1 - Wireless Usage Scenarios by Technology

Wireless Standard	Application Category	Usage Scenario
Bluetooth	WPAN Wireless Personal Area Networking	- I want to instantly connect my notebook computer to another Bluetooth enabled notebook to transfer a file. · I want to work collaboratively on a document ,where meeting participants use notebooks that are wirelessly connected via Bluetooth. · Using a Bluetooth enabled, wireless headset, I want to listen to a CD playing on my notebook computer while it is in my briefcase. · I often travel to a remote site and want to walk up to a shared printer, connect and print a document without having to physically connect using a standard printer cable. · I want to connect to the Internet via a cellular phone without having to take my telephone out of my briefcase
WiFi	WLAN Wireless Local Area Networking	· I want to always be connected to my corporate LAN while moving about in my office building or campus. · Usage demands that I have access to corporate network data at performance levels equivalent to a wire based LAN connection.
Cellular Technology (GSM)	WWAN Wireless Wide Area Networking	· I want access to email and web resources while traveling away from the home office.

Bluetooth and 802.11 are emerging as the preferred technology in the commercial space for WPAN and WLAN respectively. Higher throughput, longer range and other characteristics make 802.11 better suited for WLAN than Bluetooth. The rest of this document gives a basic overview of these two technologies detailing the basic concepts, the principles of operations, and some of the reasons behind some of their features.

3. WIRELESS LAN AND 802.11 WIFI

A wireless LAN (WLAN) is a data transmission system designed to provide location-independent network access between computing devices by using radio waves rather than a cable infrastructure [2].

In the corporate enterprise, wireless LANs are usually implemented as the final link between the existing wired network and a group of client computers, giving these users wireless access to the full resources and services of the corporate network across a building or campus setting.

The widespread acceptance of WLANs depends on industry standardization to ensure product compatibility and reliability among the various manufacturers.

The 802.11 specification[3] as a standard for wireless LANS was ratified

---

[2] "IEEE 802.11b Wireless LANs - Cs.colorado.edu."
https://www.cs.colorado.edu/~rhan/CSCI_7143_002_Fall_2001/Papers/IEEE_802_11b.pdf. Accessed 7 Nov. 2017.
[3] "Local and Metropolitan Area Networks, 2005. LANMAN ... - IEEE Xplore."
http://ieeexplore.ieee.org/xpl/mostRecentIssue.jsp?punumber=10349. Accessed

by the Institute of Electrical and Electronics Engineers (IEEE) in the year 1997. This version of 802.11 provides for 1 Mbps and 2 Mbps data rates and a set of fundamental signaling methods and other services. Like all IEEE 802 standards, the 802.11 standards focus on the bottom two levels the ISO model, the physical layer and link layer (Figure 7).

Any LAN application, network operating system, protocol, including TCP/IP and Novell NetWare, will run on an 802.11-compliant WLAN as easily as they run over Ethernet.

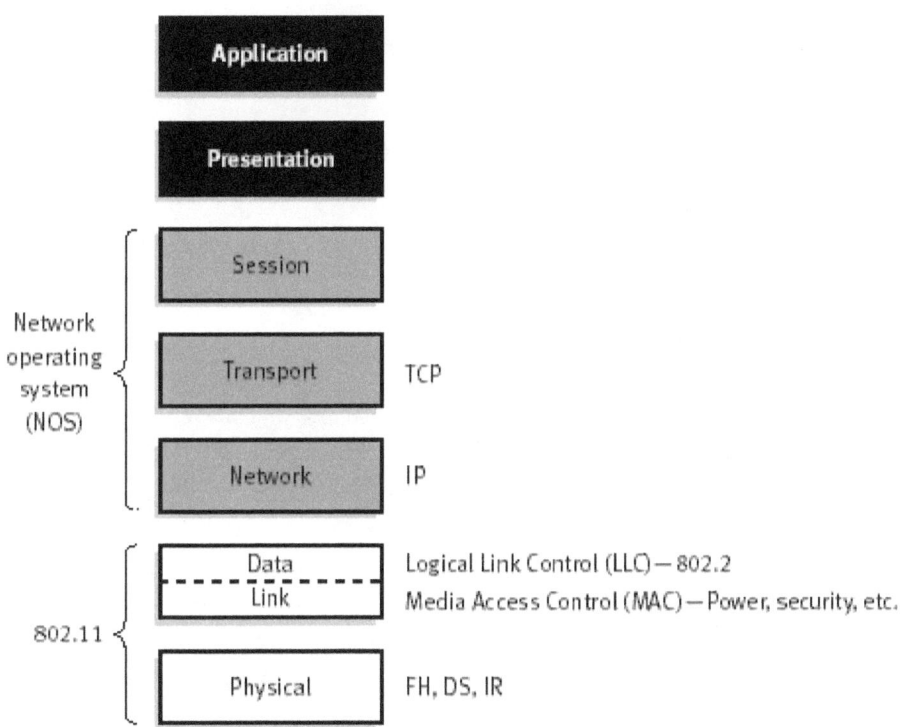

Figure 7: 802.11 and the ISO Model

gordon.colbach@cloudversity.com

4. MOTIVATION FOR WLAN

The major motivation and benefit from wireless LANs is increased mobility. Untethered from conventional network connections, network users can move about almost without restriction and access LANs from nearly anywhere.

The other advantages for WLAN include cost-effective network setup for hard-to-wire locations such as older buildings and solid-wall structures and reduced cost of ownership-particularly in dynamic environments requiring frequent modifications -thanks to minimal wiring and installation costs per device and user.

WLANs liberate users from dependence on hard-wired access to the network backbone, giving them anytime, anywhere network access. This freedom to roam offers numerous user benefits for a variety of work environments, such as:

- Immediate bedside access to patient information for doctors and hospital staff

- Easy, real-time network access for on-site consultants or auditors

- Improved database access for roving supervisors such as production line managers, warehouse auditors, or construction engineers

- Simplified network configuration with minimal MIS involvement for temporary setups such as trade shows or conference rooms

- Faster access to customer information for service vendors and retailers, resulting in better service and improved customer satisfaction

- Location-independent access for network administrators, for easier

23

on-site troubleshooting and support

- Real-time access to study group meetings and research links for students.

5. THE 802.11 ARCHITECTURE

Each computer, mobile, portable or fixed, is referred to as a station in 802.11 [4]. The difference between a portable and mobile station is that a portable station moves from point to point but is only used at a fixed point. Mobile stations access the LAN during movement.

When two or more stations come together to communicate with each other, they form a Basic Service Set (BSS). The minimum BSS consists of two stations. 802.11 LANs use the BSS as the standard building block.

A BSS that stands alone and is not connected to a base is called an Independent Basic Service Set (IBSS) or is referred to as an Ad-Hoc Network. An ad-hoc network is a network where stations communicate only peer to peer. There is no base and no one gives permission to talk.

Mostly these networks are spontaneous and can be set up rapidly. Ad-Hoc or IBSS networks are characteristically limited both temporally and spatially.

---

[4] "In-building Wireless LANs." http://www.cse.wustl.edu/~jain/cis788-99/ftp/wireless_lans.pdf. Accessed 7 Nov. 2017.

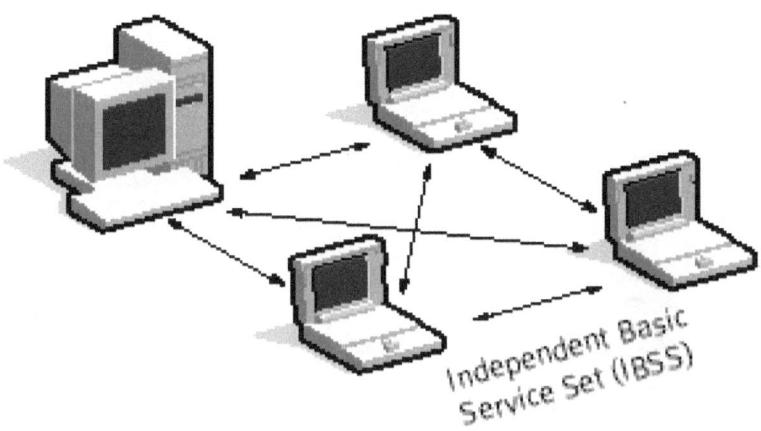

Figure 8: Adhoc Mode

When BSS's are interconnected the network becomes one with infrastructure. 802.11 infrastructure has several elements. Two or more BSS are interconnected using a Distribution System or DS.

This concept of DS increases network coverage. Each BSS becomes a component of an extended, larger network. Entry to the DS is accomplished with the use of Access Points (AP). An access point is a station, thus addressable. So, data moves between the BSS and the DS with the help of these access points.

Creating large and complex networks using BSS and DS's leads us to the next level of hierarchy, the Extended Service Set or ESS. The beauty of the ESS is the entire network looks like an independent basic service set to the Logical Link Control layer (LLC). This means that stations within the ESS can communicate or even move between BSS's transparently to the LLC.

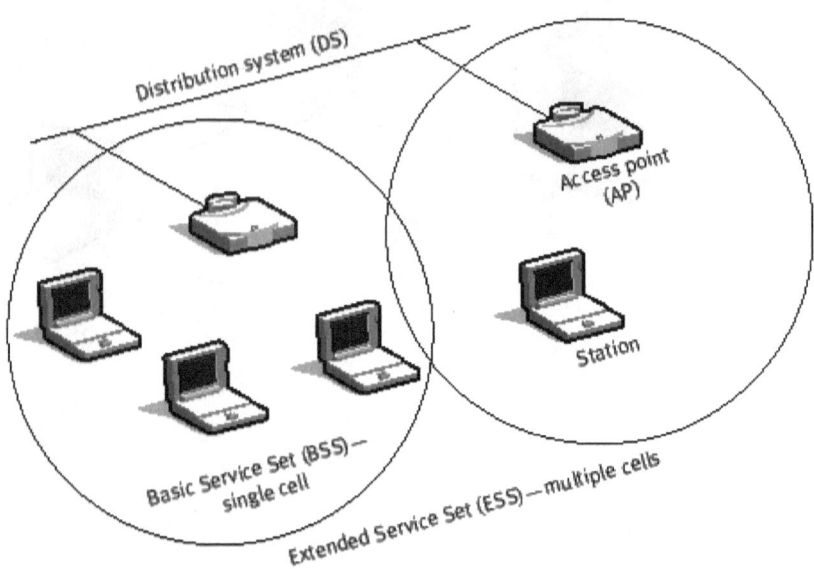

Figure 9: Infrastructure Mode

One of the requirements of IEEE 802.11 is that it can be used with existing wired networks. 802.11 solved this challenge with the use of a Portal. A portal is the logical integration between wired LANs and 802.11. It also can serve as the access point to the DS. All data going to an 802.11 LAN from an 802.X LAN must pass through a portal. It thus functions as a bridge between wired and wireless.

The implementation of the DS is not specified by 802.11. Therefore, a distribution system may be created from existing or new technologies. A point-to-point bridge connecting LANs in two separate buildings could become a DS.

While the implementation for the DS is not specified, 802.11 does specify the services, which the DS must support. Services are divided into two sections

1. Station Services (SS)
2. Distribution System Services (DSS)

There are five services provided by the DSS

1. Association
2. Reassociation
3. Disassociation
4. Distribution
5. Integration

The first three services deal with station mobility. If a station is moving within its own BSS or is not moving, the stations mobility is termed No-transition. If a station moves between BSS's within the same ESS, its mobility is termed BSS-transition. If the station moves between BSS's of differing ESS's it is ESS transition.

A station must affiliate itself with the BSS infrastructure if it wants to use the LAN. This is done by Associating itself with an access point. Associations are dynamic in nature because stations move, turn on or turn off. A station can only be associated with one AP. This ensures that the DS always knows where the station is.

Association supports no-transition mobility but is not enough to support BSS-transition. Enter Reassociation. This service allows the station to switch its association from one AP to another. Both association and reassociation are initiated by the station.

Disassociation is when the association between the station and the AP is terminated. This can be initiated by either party. A disassociated station cannot send or receive data. ESS-transition are not supported. A station can move to a new ESS but will have to reinitiate connections.

Distribution and Integration are the remaining DSS's. Distribution is simply getting the data from the sender to the intended receiver. The message is sent to the local AP (input AP), then distributed through the DS to the AP (output AP) that the recipient is associated with. If the sender and receiver are in the same BSS, the input and out AP's are the same. So the distribution service is logically invoked whether the data is going through the DS or not. Integration is when the output AP is a portal. Thus, 802.x LANs are integrated into the 802.11 DS.

Station services are:

1. Authentication
2. Deauthentication
3. Privacy
4. MAC Service Data Unit (MSDU) Delivery.

With a wireless system, the medium is not exactly bounded as with a wired system. In order to control access to the network, stations must first establish their identity. This is much like trying to enter a radio net in the military.

Before you are acknowledged and allowed to converse, you must first pass a series of tests to ensure that you are who you say you are. That is really all authentication is. Once a station has been authenticated, it may then associate itself. The authentication relationship may be between two stations inside an IBSS or to the AP of the BSS. Authentication outside of the BSS does not take place.

There are two types of authentication services offered by 802.11. The first is Open System Authentication. This means that anyone who attempts to authenticate will receive authentication. The second type is Shared Key Authentication. In order to become authenticated the users must be in possession of a shared secret. The shared secret is implemented with the use of the Wired Equivalent Privacy (WEP) privacy algorithm. The shared secret is delivered to all stations ahead of time in some secure method (such as someone walking around and loading the secret onto each station).

Deauthentication is when either the station or AP wishes to terminate a stations authentication. When this happens the station is automatically disassociated.

Privacy is an encryption algorithm, which is used so that other 802.11 users cannot eavesdrop on your LAN traffic. IEEE 802.11 specifies Wired Equivalent Privacy (WEP) as an optional algorithm to satisfy privacy. If WEP is not used then stations are "in the clear" or "in the red", meaning that their traffic is not encrypted. Data transmitted in the clear are called plaintext. Data transmissions, which are encrypted, are called ciphertext.

All stations start "in the red" until they are authenticated. MSDU delivery ensures that the information in the MAC service data unit is delivered between the medium access control service access points.

The bottom line is this, authentication is basically a network wide password. Privacy is whether or not encryption is used. Wired Equivalent Privacy is used to protect authorized stations from eavesdroppers. WEP is reasonably strong. The algorithm can be broken in time. The relationship between breaking the algorithm is directly related to the length of time that a key is in use. So, WEP allows for changing of the key to prevent brute force attack of the algorithm.

WEP can be implemented in hardware or in software. One reason that WEP is optional is because encryption may not be exported from the United States. This allows 802.11 to be a standard outside the U.S. albeit without the encryption.

5.1. The 802.11 Physical Layer

The three physical layers originally defined in 802.11 included two spread-spectrum radio techniques and a diffuse infrared specification. The radio-based standards operate within the 2.4 GHz ISM band. These frequency bands are recognized by international regulatory agencies radio operations.

As such, 802.11-based products do not require user licensing or special training. Spread-spectrum techniques, in addition to satisfying regulatory requirements, increase reliability, boost throughput, and allow many unrelated products to share the spectrum without explicit cooperation and with minimal interference.

The original 802.11 wireless standard defines data rates of 1 Mbps and 2 Mbps via radio waves using frequency hopping spread spectrum (FHSS) or direct sequence spread spectrum (DSSS). It is important to note that FHSS and DSSS are fundamentally different signaling mechanisms and will not interoperate with one another. Using the frequency hopping technique, the 2.4 GHz band is divided into 75 1-MHz subchannels.

The sender and receiver agree on a hopping pattern, and data is sent over a sequence of the subchannels. Each conversation within the 802.11 network occurs over a different hopping pattern, and the patterns are designed to minimize the chance of two senders using the same subchannel simultaneously.

FHSS techniques allow for a relatively simple radio design, but are limited to speeds of no higher than 2 Mbps. This limitation is driven primarily by FCC (Federal Communications Commission USA) regulations that restrict subchannel bandwidth to 1 MHz. These regulations force FHSS systems to spread their usage across the entire 2.4 GHz band, meaning they must hop often, which leads to a high amount of hopping overhead.

In contrast, the direct sequence signaling technique divides the 2.4 GHz band into 14 22-MHz channels. Adjacent channels overlap one another partially, with three of the 14 being completely non-overlapping. Data is sent across one of these 22 MHz channels without hopping to other channels. To compensate for noise on a given channel, a technique called "chipping" is used.

Each bit of user data is converted into a series of redundant bit patterns called "chips." The inherent redundancy of each chip combined with spreading the signal across the 22 MHz channel provides for a form of error checking and correction; even if part of the signal is damaged, it can still be recovered in many cases, minimizing the need for retransmissions.

5.2. The 802.11 Data Link Layer

The data link layer within 802.11 consists of two sublayers: Logical Link Control (LLC) and Media Access Control (MAC). 802.11 uses the same 802.2 LLC and 48-bit addressing as other 802 LANs, allowing for very simple bridging from wireless to IEEE wired networks, but the MAC is unique to WLANs.

The 802.11 MAC is very similar in concept to 802.3, in that it is designed to support multiple users on a shared medium by having the sender sense the medium before accessing it. For 802.3 Ethernet LANs, the Carrier Sense Multiple Access with Collision Detection (CSMA/CD) protocol regulates how Ethernet stations establish access to the wire and how they detect and handle collisions that occur when two or more devices try to simultaneously communicate over the LAN.

In an 802.11 WLAN, collision detection is not possible due to what is known as the "near/far" problem: to detect a collision, a station must be able to transmit and listen at the same time, but in radio systems the transmission drowns out the ability of the station to "hear" a collision.

To account for this difference, 802.11 uses a slightly modified protocol known as Carrier Sense Multiple Access with Collision Avoidance (CSMA/CA) or the Distributed Coordination Function (DCF). CSMA/CA attempts to avoid collisions by using explicit packet acknowledgment (ACK), which means an ACK packet is sent by the receiving station to confirm that the data packet arrived intact.

CSMA/CA works as follows. A station wishing to transmit senses the air, and, if no activity is detected, the station waits an additional, randomly selected period of time and then transmits if the medium is still free. If the packet is received intact, the receiving station issues an ACK frame that, once successfully received by the sender, completes the process.

If the ACK frame is not detected by the sending station, either because the original data packet was not received intact or the ACK was not received intact, a collision is assumed to have occurred and the data packet is transmitted again after waiting another random amount of time.

CSMA/CA thus provides a way of sharing access over the air. This explicit ACK mechanism also handles interference and other radio related problems very effectively. However, it does add some overhead to 802.11 that 802.3 does not have, so that an 802.11 LAN will always have slower performance than an equivalent Ethernet LAN.

Another MAC-layer problem specific to wireless is the "hidden node" issue, in which two stations on opposite sides of an access point can both "hear" activity from an access point, but not from each other, usually due to distance or an obstruction.

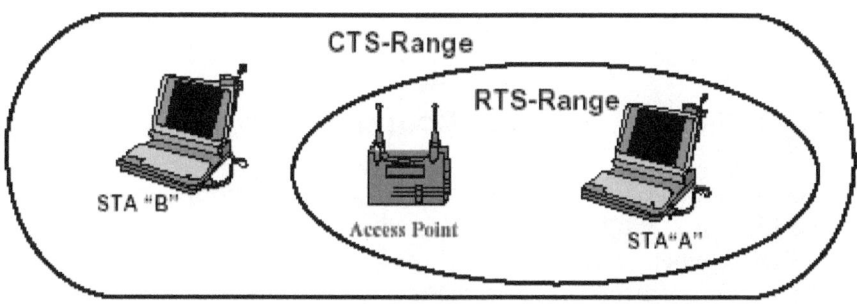

Figure 10: RTS/CTS Procedure eliminates the 'Hidden Node' Problem

To solve this problem, 802.11 specifies an optional Request to Send/Clear to Send (RTS/CTS) protocol at the MAC layer. When this feature is in use, a sending station transmits an RTS and waits for the access point to reply with a CTS.

Since all stations in the network can hear the access point, the CTS causes them to delay any intended transmissions, allowing the sending station to transmit and receive a packet acknowledgment without any chance of collision.

Since RTS/CTS adds additional overhead to the network by temporarily reserving the medium, it is typically used only on the largest-sized packets, for which retransmission would be expensive from a bandwidth standpoint.

Finally, the 802.11 MAC layer provides for two other robustness features: CRC checksum and packet fragmentation. Each packet has a CRC checksum calculated and attached to ensure that the data was not corrupted in transit.

This is different from Ethernet, where higher-level protocols such as TCP handle error checking. Packet fragmentation allows large packets to be broken into smaller units when sent over the air, which is useful in very congested environments or when interference is a factor, since larger packets have a better chance of being corrupted.

This technique reduces the need for retransmission in many cases and thus improves overall wireless network performance. The MAC layer is responsible for reassembling fragments received, rendering the process transparent to higher level protocols.

5.2.1. Support for Time-Bounded Data

Time-bounded data such as voice and video is supported in the 802.11 MAC specification through the Point Coordination Function (PCF). As opposed to the DCF, where control is distributed to all stations, in PCF mode a single access point controls access to the media. If a BSS is set up with PCF enabled, time is spliced between the system being in PCF mode and in DCF (CSMA/CA) mode.

During the periods when the system is in PCF mode, the access point will poll each station for data, and after a given time move on to the next station. No station is allowed to transmit unless it is polled, and stations receive data from the access point only when they are polled. Since PCF gives every station a turn to transmit in a predetermined fashion, a maximum latency is guaranteed.

A downside to PCF is that it is not particularly scalable, in that a single point needs to have control of media access and must poll all stations, which can be ineffective in large networks.

6. SECURITY IN 802.11

Security is one of the first concerns of people deploying a Wireless LAN, the 802.11 committee has addressed the issue by providing what is called WEP (Wired Equivalent Privacy)[5].

The main concerns of users are that an intruder would not be able to:

- Access the Network resources by using similar Wireless LAN equipment, and
- Be able to capture the Wireless LAN traffic (eavesdropping)

Preventing Access to Network Resources

This is done by the use of an Authentication mechanism where a station needs to prove knowledge of the current key; this is very similar to the Wired LAN privacy, in the sense that an intruder needs to enter the premises (by using a physical key) in order to connect his workstation to the wired LAN.

Eavesdropping

---

[5] "A Technical Tutorial on the IEEE 802.11 Protocol." 18 Jul. 1996, http://www.sss-mag.com/pdf/802_11tut.pdf. Accessed 7 Nov. 2017.

Eavesdropping is prevented by the use of the WEP algorithm, which is a Pseudo Random Number Generator (PRNG), initialized by a shared secret key. This PRNG outputs a key sequence of pseudo-random bits equal in length to the largest possible packet, which is combined with the outgoing/incoming packet producing the packet transmitted in the air.

The WEP algorithm is a simple algorithm based on RSA's RC4 algorithm, which has the following properties:

1. **Reasonably strong**: Brute-force attack to this algorithm is difficult because of the fact that every frame is sent with an Initialization Vector, which restarts the PRNG for each frame.

2. **Self Synchronizing**: The algorithm synchronized again for each message, this is needed in order to work on a connectionless environment, where packets may get lost (as any LAN).

7. 802.11 STANDARDS

The most critical issue affecting WLAN demand had been limited throughput. The data rates supported by the original 802.11 standard were too slow to support most general business requirements and slowed the adoption of WLANs.

Recognizing the critical need to support higher data-transmission rates, the IEEE ratified the **802.11b** standard (also known as 802.11 High Rate) for transmissions of up to **11 Mbps**.

After 802.11b one more standard **802.11a** was ratified which took the transmission speed upto **54 Mbps**, though it used the less crowded **5 GHz** band to transport.

The letters after the number "802.11" tell us the order in which the standards were first proposed. This means that the "new" 802.11a is actually older than the currently used 802.11b, which just happened to be ready first because it was based on relatively simple technology-Direct Sequence Spread Spectrum (DSSS), as opposed to 802.11a' Orthogonal Frequency Division Multiplexing (OFDM). The more complex technology provides a higher data rate: 802.11b can reach 11 Mbits/sec, while 802.11a can reach 54 Mbits/sec.

Around **June 2003**, the next generation **802.11g** was announced and it bought the **54 Mbps** speeds possible in 802.11a in the 5 GHz band to the original **2.4 GHz** band.

802.11n was published around **October 2009** and added **MIMO** (multiple-input multiple-output) antenna support. MIMO allows the usage of multiple antennas at both the source and destination and improved the maximum data rates to around **600 Mbit/s**.

In **Dec 2013** the next upgrade to 802.11 came in the form of **802.11ac** and provided theoretical improved rates to around **7 Gbps**. The 802.11ac upgrades were launched in a staggered manner to enabled devices and are known as **802.11ac Wave 1** and **802.11ac Wave 2** respectively.

The future upgrade to 802.11 is known as **802.11ax** and has been tested to reach connection speeds exceeding **10 Gbps**. 802.11ax is still in development though and ratification is expected around **2019**.

7.1. 802.11 b

With 802.11b WLANs, mobile users can get Ethernet levels of performance, throughput, and availability. The basic architecture, features, and services of 802.11b are defined by the original 802.11 standard. The 802.11b specification affects only the physical layer, adding higher data rates and more robust connectivity.

The key contribution of the 802.11b addition to the wireless LAN standard was to standardize the physical layer support of two new speeds,5.5 Mbps and 11 Mbps. To accomplish this, DSSS had to be selected as the sole physical layer technique for the standard since, as frequency hopping cannot support the higher speeds without violating current FCC regulations. The implication is that 802.11b systems will interoperate with 1 Mbps and 2 Mbps 802.11 DSSS systems, but will not work with 1 Mbps and 2 Mbps 802.11 FHSS systems.

The original 802.11 DSSS standard specifies an 11-bit chipping-called a Barker sequence-to encode all data sent over the air. Each 11-chip sequence represents a single data bit (1 or 0), and is converted to a waveform, called a symbol, that can be sent over the air. These symbols are transmitted at a 1 MSps (1 million symbols per second) symbol rate using technique called Binary Phase Shift Keying (BPSK).

In the case of 2 Mbps, a more sophisticated implementation called Quadrature Phase Shift Keying (QPSK) is used; it doubles the data rate available in BPSK, via improved efficiency in the use of the radio bandwidth. To increase the data rate in the 802.11b standard, advanced coding techniques are employed.

Rather than the two 11-bit Barker sequences, 802.11b specifies Complementary Code Keying (CCK), which consists of a set of 64 8-bit code words. As a set, these code words have unique mathematical properties that allow them to be correctly distinguished from one another by a receiver even in the presence of substantial noise and multipath interference (e.g., interference caused by receiving multiple radio reflections within a building).

The 5.5 Mbps rate uses CCK to encode 4 bits per carrier, while the 11 Mbps rate encodes 8 bits per carrier. Both speeds use QPSK as the modulation technique and signal at 1.375 MSps. This is how the higher data rates are obtained.

To support very noisy environments as well as extended range, 802.11b WLANs use dynamic rate shifting, allowing data rates to be automatically adjusted to compensate for the changing nature of the radio channel. Ideally, users connect at the full 11 Mbps rate.

However when devices move beyond the optimal range for 11 Mbps operation, or if substantial interference is present, 802.11b devices will transmit at lower speeds, falling back to 5.5, 2, and 1 Mbps.

Likewise, if the device moves back within the range of a higher-speed transmission, the connection will automatically speed up again. Rate shifting is a physical layer mechanism transparent to the user and the upper layers of the protocol stack.

One of the more significant disadvantages of 802.11b is that the frequency band is crowded, and subject to interference from other networking technologies, microwave ovens, 2.4GHz cordless phones (a huge market), and Bluetooth [6].

There are drawbacks to 802.11b, including lack of interoperability with voice devices, and no QoS provisions for multimedia content. Interference and other limitations aside, 802.11b is the clear leader in business and institutional wireless networking and is gaining share for home applications as well.

---

[6] "Wireless Standards Up in the Air - ExtremeTech." 3 Dec. 2001, https://www.extremetech.com/computing/71924-wireless-standards-up-in-the-air. Accessed 7 Nov. 2017.

7.2. 802.11 a

802.11a, with a **54Mbps** maximum data rate, is much faster than 802.11b and operates in the **5GHz** frequency range allowing for eight simultaneous channels [7]. 802.11a uses **Orthogonal Frequency Division Multiplexing** **(OFDM)**, a new encoding scheme that offers benefits over spread spectrum in channel availability and data rate.

Channel availability is significant because the more independent channels that are available, the more scalable the wireless network becomes. 802.11a uses OFDM to define a total of 8 non-overlapping 20MHz channels across the 2 lower bands. By comparison, 802.11b uses 3 non-overlapping channels.

All wireless LANs use unlicensed spectrum; therefore they're prone to interference and transmission errors. To reduce errors, both types of 802.11 automatically reduce the Physical layer data rate. IEEE 802.11b has three lower data rates (5.5, 2, and 1Mbit/sec), and 802.11a has seven (48, 36, 24, 18, 12, 9, and 6 Mbits/sec). Higher (and more) data rates aren't 802.11a's only advantage. It also uses a higher frequency band, 5GHz, which is both wider and less crowded than the 2.4GHz band that 802.11b shares with cordless phones, microwave ovens, and Bluetooth devices.

The wider band means that more radio channels can coexist without interference. Each radio channel corresponds to a separate network, or a switched segment on the same network. One big disadvantage is that it is not directly compatible with 802.11b, and requires new bridging products that can support both types of networks.

---

[7] "EMERGING TECHNOLOGIES Wireless Networks - Language ...."
http://llt.msu.edu/vol6num1/pdf/emerging.pdf. Accessed 7 Nov. 2017.

Other clear disadvantages are that 802.11a is only available in half the bandwidth in Japan (for a maximum of four channels), and it isn't approved for use in Europe, where HiperLAN 2 is the standard.

7.3. 802.11 g

Though 5GHz has many advantages, it also has problems. The most important of these is compatibility: The different frequencies mean that 802.11a products aren't interoperable with 802.11b base. To get around this, the IEEE developed 802.11g, which should extend the speed and range of 802.11b so that it's fully compatible with the older systems.

The standard operates entirely in the 2.4GHz frequency, but uses a minimum of two modes (both mandatory) with two optional modes [8]. The mandatory modulation/access modes are the same CCK (Complementary Code Keying) mode used by 802.11b (hence the compatibility) and OFDM (Orthogonal Frequency Division Multiplexing) mode used by 802.11a (but in this case in the 2.4GHz frequency band).

The mandatory CCK mode supports 11 Mbps and the OFDM mode has a maximum of 54Mbps. There are also two modes that use different methods to attain a 22 Mbps data rate--PBCC-22 (Packet Binary Convolutional Coding, rated for 6 to 54Mbps) and CCK-OFDM mode (with a rated max of 33Mbps).

The obvious advantage of 802.11g is that it maintains compatibility with 802.11b (and 802.11b's worldwide acceptance) and also offers faster data rates comparable with 802.11a. The number of channels available, however, is not increased, since channels are a function of bandwidth, not radio signal modulation - and on that score, 802.11a wins with its eight channels, compared to the three channels available with either 802.11b or 802.11g.

Another disadvantage of 802.11g is that it also works in the 2.4 GHz band and so due to interference it will never be as fast as 802.11a

---

[8] "Wireless Standards Up in the Air - ExtremeTech." 3 Dec. 2001, https://www.extremetech.com/computing/71924-wireless-standards-up-in-the-air. Accessed 7 Nov. 2017.

7.4. 802.11 n

The core upgrade that 802.11n provided over earlier standards was the support of what is known as **MIMO** (multiple-input, multiple-output) antenna.

Coupled with the addition of wider **40 MHz** channel widths (as opposed to 20 MHz in the earlier version) this resulted the maximum data rates to about **600 Mbit/s** from the 54 Mbit/s possible over 802.11 a and g. [9]

802.11n was published in **October 2009** and also included support for frame aggregation, improved interoperability with legacy standards and security upgrades along with other features.

7.4.1. MIMO

MIMO(multiple-input, multiple-output) allowed for the multiplexing of multiple independent data streams within one spectral channel of Bandwidth. This is called **Spatial Division Multiplexing (SDM)**, supports upto 3 different data streams within a single channel and can dramatically increase data throughput with each additional stream.

The only caveat being that each of these data streams needs to be supported by an independent antenna at both the transmitter and the receiver. This puts an obvious constraint in the interoperability of 802.11n with earlier versions of the standard as both devices need to support multiple antennas to support increased speeds.

7.4.2. 40 MHz Channels

The other key upgrade of 802.11 n was the support of 40 MHz channels. This earlier versions of 802.11 standards limited to channels widths of only 20 MHz. This effectively doubles the theoretical PHY data rate over a single channel and coupled with MIMO allowed for 802.11n to roughly grow the

---

[9] "IEEE 802.11n-2009 - Wikipedia."
https://en.wikipedia.org/wiki/IEEE_802.11n-2009. Accessed 18 Apr. 2018.

theoretical maximum data rate 10 times (over 802.11a/g) to around **600 Mbit/s**.

In practice however a radio might not be able to utilize each available antenna to transmit a unique data stream. Radios are themselves limited by the number of spatial streams that they can carry, and hence the minimum of this number and the antennas available is what determines the practical multiplexing rate possible.

The radio capability is denoted in the **a x b : c** notation:
1. 'a' denotes the number of transmit antennas that the radio has access to
2. 'b' denotes the number of receive antennas that the radio has access to
3. 'c' denotes the underlying capability of the radio to support independent data streams.

So for example, a radio that can send on 3 antennas, receive on 2 antennas but can only support 2 antennas would be noted as: **3 x 2 : 2** . This radio can support 2 independent data streams but only when the other side can also support a minimum of 2.

Even though the 802.11n draft allowed for upto 4 x 4 : 4 configurations but most 802.11n devices support either of the following three configurations:
1. 2 x 2 : 2
2. 2 x 3 : 2
3. 3 x 2 : 2

Note that each of the configuration above has the same maximum throughput enabled by a maximum of 2 independent data streams per channel. Another configuration which is now being increasingly supported is 3 x 3 : 3 and has a higher throughput due to the support of 3 independent data streams per channel.

7.4.3. Frame aggregation

Frame aggregation features in 802.11n seeks to improve user level throughput by bunding the protocol level overheads together and averaging them over multiple frames. The protocol overheads might include information about the contention rate, interframe spacing, PHY level headers and acknowledgement frames.

Media Access Control(MAC) provides for two types of aggregation:

1. A-MSDU: Aggregation of MAC service data units (MSDU) at the top of the MAC
2. A-MPDU: Aggregation of MAC protocol data units (MPDU) at the bottom of the MAC.

7.4.4. Throughput Optimization

An 802.11g network operating on a single 20 MHz channel and one antenna can achieve 54 Mbps. An equivalent 802.11n network operating under similar conditions can do around 72 Mbps.

However, 802.11n allows for the usage of two 20 MHz channels in the 40 MHz mode and theoretically double the date rate to around 150 Mbps. The real life output might vary depending on how much contention exists in the 2.4 GHz spectrum due to other Bluetooth, microwave or WiFi emissions in the vicinity.

Now if we increase the antennas to the maximum of 4 as provided by 802.11n, we can increase our data rate 4 times to around 600 Mbps. Note that we are still using the 40 MHz spectrum which might see congestion in a most practical settings and especially in urban areas. Consequently real life installations in urban areas might benefit from providing satisfactory bandwidth even on 20 MHz mode

An addition level to maximize throughput would be to use the 5 GHz network. The 5 GHz network is relatively less congested as compared to the 2.4 GHz band and provides for many non-overlapping radio channels with substantially reduced interference.

Most real life installations would also need to support legacy equipment that is still on 802.11 b/g. So an optimal solution might use a dual-radio access point and place the 802.11 b/g traffic on the 2.4 GHz radio and the 802.11n traffic on the 5 GHz radio.

Some enterprise grade Access Points also do what has come to be known as **'band steering'**. Access points implement band steering by selective responding to only 5 GHz association request from dual band enabled clients. This results in the usage of 5 GHz bands for all 802.11n enabled clients while leaving the 2.4 GHz band open for devices supporting legacy protocols.

7.5. 802.11 ac

IEEE 802.11 ac was launched in December **2013** and boosted the theoretical maximum data rates to almost **7 Gbps** over the 600 Mbps possible in 802.11n.

The actual support of 802.11ac in devices has been staggered with what has come to be known as **Wave 1** and **Wave 2** rollouts. While Wave 1 pushed the maximum data rates to around 1.3 Gbps, Wave 2 implemented the rest of the feature set taking the speeds to 6.93 Gbps.

Figure: 802.11 ac router

802.11ac increased data rates by broadly using the following feature set:

1. **MU-MIMO (multi-user MIMO)**: MU-MIMO is an upgrade over MIMO introduced with 802.11n and allows for one 11ac device to transmit individual data streams to multiple devices at the same time.
2. **More Spatial Streams**: 802.11ac further increased the maximum possible spatial streams over a single channel to 4.
3. **Wider Channels**: 802.11n had increased the channel width to 40

MHz from the 20 MHz possible in the earlier protocols. 802.11ac further increased this limit to allow for 80 MHz and 160 MHz channels.

Each of these upgrades were introduced to user devices in a staggered manner through Wave 1 and Wave 2.

7.5.1. Wave 1

The first Wave 1 products were introduced to the market in 2013. The key protocol upgrades launched as a part of Wave 1 included:

1. 80 MHz channels
2. 3 Spatial Streams
3. No MU-MIMO - Multi-user MIMO support was not launched as a part of Wave 1.

Each of these upgrades combined together to push the maximum data rates to around 1.3 Gbps over the 600 Mbps possible with 802.11n

7.5.2. Wave 2

Wave 2 devices have started appearing in the market starting from late 2014. Wave 2 saw the first implementation of MU-MIMO capability outlined in the protocol. The supporting protocol upgrades launched as part of Wave 2 included:

1. 160 MHz channels
2. 4 Spatial Streams
3. MU-MIMO

With the 160 MHz bonding to 4 spatial data streams enabled on a MU-MIMO capable radio, the Wave 2 devices have pushed the data rate to around **6.93 Gbps**.

7.6. 802.11 ax

802.11 ax is the future upgrade over 802.11 ac and is targeted for a **2019** launch. Even though 802.11 ax will offer only incremental upgrades to the maximum data rates, the user level throughput is expected jump four-fold on the back of more efficient spectrum utilization scheme.

The increased spectral efficiency is primarily due to a new modulation scheme called **OFDMA** (Orthogonal Frequency Division Multiple Access)[10] with a denser constellation **1024-QAM** modulation scheme.[11]

OFDMA is a multi-user version of the popular OFDM (orthogonal frequency division multiplexing) digital modulation scheme. OFDMA works by assigning subsets of subcarriers to individual users to allow for low-data-rate transmission from multiple users at the same time.

802.11 ax will piggy back both of these upgrades on the top of MU-MIMO which was introduced as part of 802.11 ac Wave 2 devices.

Implementations of 802.11 ax have already started appearing on the market and CES 2018 showcased devices which reached around **11 Gbps** throughput.[12]

---

[10] "Orthogonal frequency-division multiple access - Wikipedia." https://en.wikipedia.org/wiki/Orthogonal_frequency-division_multiple_access. Accessed 18 Apr. 2018.
[11] "Quadrature amplitude modulation - Wikipedia." https://en.wikipedia.org/wiki/Quadrature_amplitude_modulation. Accessed 18 Apr. 2018.
[12] "D-Link, Asus tout 802.11ax Wi-Fi routers, but you'll have to ... - ZDNet." 8 Jan. 2018, https://www.zdnet.com/article/d-link-asus-tout-802-11ax-wi-fi-routers-but-youll-have-to-wait-until-later-in-2018/. Accessed 18 Apr. 2018.

8. Future Amendments to 802.11

There are two key organizations working towards the development of 802.11 standards and commercialization of 802.11 for consumer LAN devices. These are the IEEE 802.11[13] and Wi-Fi Alliance[14] respectively.

IEEE 802.11 specifies the standards and protocols for the 802.11 technology, and the Wi-Fi Alliance complements this work by providing specifications for extended functionality and interoperability requirements for different equipment providers and the broad wireless industry.

The charter for Wi-Fi Alliance is to commercialize the technologies specified by the core IEEE 802.11 standard by connecting the specification to consumer devices. Wi-Fi Alliance is tasked with making Wi-Fi practical and usable by ensuring interoperability compliance amongst different devices manufactured by wireless manufacturers.

The Wi-Fi Alliance works across a broad application categories of Wi-Fi. This includes but is not limited to:

1. Automotive
2. Frequency management and band-steering
3. Mesh networks
4. Service discovery and optimization

---

[13] "IEEE 802.11, The Working Group Setting the Standards for ...." http://www.ieee802.org/11/. Accessed 9 Oct. 2019.
[14] "Wi-Fi Alliance." https://www.wi-fi.org/. Accessed 9 Oct. 2019.

5.   Internet of Things technology
6.   Convergent solutions with 4G and 5G

To make the 802.11 standards easier for the consumers to understand, the Wi-Fi Alliance has recently renamed the IEEE nomenclature to make it more user friendly.

The revised nomenclature starts from 802.11 b, which is now attractively named Wi-Fi 1. It goes up to 802.11 ax, which is now also renamed Wi-Fi 6. The previous version is 802.11 ac, which is now renamed as Wi-Fi 5.

However not all 802.11 standards have been given simpler names. So the other standards that are not defined under this nomenclature will still be known by their original IEEE nomenclature. Also these names are only adopted by the Wi-Fi Alliance and are consumer facing purpose only. The core IEEE organization hasn't adopted these names and will still name the specifications by their original IEEE names.

Table: IEEE Specifications and Proposed Wi-Fi Alliance names.

IEEE Designation	Wi-Fi Alliance Name
802.11 b	Wi-Fi 1
802.11 a	Wi-Fi 2
802.11 g	Wi-Fi 3
802.11 n	Wi-Fi 4
802.11 ac	Wi-Fi 5
802.11 ax	Wi-Fi 6
802.11 be (projected)	Wi-Fi 7

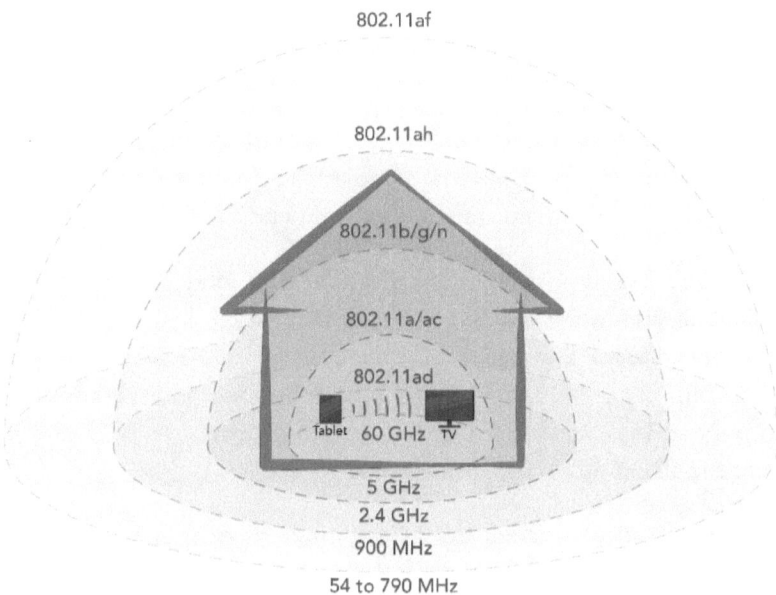

Figure: Planned updates to 802.11 with operating frequency and range.

8.1. 802.11 mc (Wi-Fi RTT)

IEEE 802.11 mc[15] was compiled by the Task Group mc (TGmc) of the IEEE 802.11 working group. The final standard is also known as IEEE 802.11 mc and was added to the main standard as an amendment in 2016.

The TGmc Group is the third revision and the group tasked with maintaining the 802.11 standard. It was formed in 2012 to incorporate additional editorial and technical connections in the 802.11 standard. The Task Group finally submitted its proposal; the additions and corrections were incorporated into the main 802.11 standard by the year 2016 and became a part of the IEEE 802.11 2016 standard.

Amendments incorporated by TGmc on top of IEEE Std 802.11-2012 include:

1. IEEE Std 802.11ae-2012
2. IEEE Std 802.11aa-2012
3. IEEE Std 802.11ad-2012
4. IEEE Std 802.11ac-2013
5. IEEE Std 802.11af-2013

TGmc ceased operations, and going forward, further revisions to the standards are now handled by the Task Group md (TGmd). The IEEE 802.11 mc has a couple of improvements on the IEEE 802.11 standard.

Wi-Fi RTT

The key improvement in 802.11 mc are the updates to the round-trip measurement times, also known as the Wi-Fi RTT (Round-Trip Time). RTT allows for an accurate measurement of location in indoor scenarios by measuring the round-trip delay time from surrounding access points. The

---

[15] "The Latest Progress on IEEE 802.11mc and IEEE 802.11ai [Standards ....]" 26 Aug. 2016, http://ieeexplore.ieee.org/document/7553423/. Accessed 9 Oct. 2019.

precision afforded in Wi-Fi RTT is to a distance of one to two meters, which is a substantial improvement over the techniques prior to 802.11. The earlier techniques were based on triangulation over the Received Signal Strength Indication (RSSI) measurement and was comparatively an order of magnitude less precise.

Triangulation requires multiple access points to pinpoint the location of the device. With a single access point, only the distance to that access point can be estimated. Triangulation requires at least three access points to accurately pinpoint the X and Y coordinates—the latitude and longitude coordinates—for any device.

802.11 mc or Wi-Fi RTT requires hardware support from the access points to enable this feature, but hardware support is not required on client devices. A firmware upgrade can provide RTT support to client devices.

Applications

The key capability that 802.11 mc enables is location awareness in indoor areas. Location awareness can yield a variety of applications that were not possible before 802.11 mc.

A very obvious requirement to make smartphones location-aware is to enable an app that responds to voice commands. For example, Alexa could switch on the lights when asked and could figure out the correct room based upon the location coordinates supplied by your smartphone.

The same capability can also be used in indoor commercial spaces. For example, shopping malls can allow easier discovery of their wares through an app that can guide you to the right location for the product you are looking for.

Another application is first-person shooting games, for example. An augmented reality location in an indoor or outdoor setting can be finetuned in 802.11 mc, enabling augmented reality based role-playing games.

Deployment

The latest version of Android - Android 9, also known as Android Pie - contains support for 802.11 mc. Applications on Android 9 can use RTT to estimate the location of the user to a precision of one to two meters. The caveat is that this requires access point hardware that supports 802.11 mc, and the app would need to get the location permission from the user to utilize the support from the OS.

The key implementation detail is that the phones are not required to connect to any access point. The phone can determine the distance by calculating the RTT from multiple access points, and this does not require an authentication or a full connection to be established with the access point.

Under the hood is Google keeps a geolocation database of access points and their location. These locations are then used to triangulate the client device location based upon the RTT. Each of the access points is identified by its MAC address, and the Google geolocation database is queried to figure out its position. The location Application Programming Interface (API) provided by Android further triangulates the client device location based upon the distances calculated from each RTT and the geolocation database cached location of each of the access points.

The other key detail is that this would typically require access to the Internet, if not from those access points through which the client device picks out the location then from a 4G/5G network that can be used to query Google's geolocation database.

The entire implementation of the geolocation database, the querying of the individual access point locations, and the further calculation of the client device location using RTT is provided as an API in Android 9.

In the event of no internet connection, the client device can also figure out and triangulate its position if the real-world location of the access point is known. So, for example, if there is an indoor location with at least three access points, their locations can be queried and stored in the client device. The client device can further triangulate its location with respect to the access point based upon this internal database.

8.2. 802.11 ad (Wi-Gig)

802.11 ad[16] is also known as Wi-Gig. Wi-Gig was announced in the year 2009 and was finally added to the IEEE 802.11 family in December 2012.

Wi-Gig defines a new physical layer for 802.11 networks to operate in the 60 gigahertz (GHz) millimeter wave spectrum. The 60 GHz millimeter wave spectrum has significantly different propagation characteristics, compared to the 2.4 and 5 GHz bands used by traditional Wi-Fi devices.

Although this allows a very high transmission rate of up to around 7 gigabits per second (Gbps), Wi-Gig is limited to work only in short distances - anywhere from 1 to 10 meters. 802.11 ad was meant to be a fiber optic replacement that can achieve speeds near to what is possible in fiber optic cables in a local LAN setting.

Even though 802.11 ad was approved in 2012, it hasn't really taken off in the market, This is primarily because of two reasons. First, the requirement for high bandwidth transmission at 7 Gbps and very short communication range isn't a key requirement for many applications.

The applications 802.11 ad was targeted for included video streaming and heavy downloads, and the current Wi-Fi standards seem to have taken care of this requirement pretty well. The second issue with 802.11 ad is that the chips are very expensive to manufacture which makes this a very costly setup.

Because of the lack of clearly defined applications and the high cost involved, 802.11 ad hasn't really taken off in a big way.

---

[16] "IEEE 802.11ad-2012 - IEEE Standard for Information ...." 28 Dec. 2012, https://standards.ieee.org/standard/802_11ad-2012.html. Accessed 10 Oct. 2019.

8.3. 802.11 af (White-Fi)

IEEE 802.11 af [17] is also known as White-Fi or super Wi-Fi. 802.11 af was approved in February 2014 and added to the IEEE 802.11 standard. The key difference between af and previous Wi-Fi standards is that 802.11 af allows a wireless LAN operation in the TV white space spectrum in the VHF and UHF bands.

The VHF and UHF bands are present between 54 MHz and 790 MHz frequency bandwidth. The key advantage for propagation of wireless LAN in these bands is that it increases the possible range as compared to traditional Wi-Fi operating at higher frequency bands. The other difference is that transmitting at a lower frequency band allows much less attenuation by materials such as brick and concrete and therefore increases the range in indoor spaces and buildings.

The 802.11 af standard recognizes that the UHF and VHF spectrums are primarily used by analog/digital TV's or wireless microphones; hence it provides the ability to reduce interference with these primary uses while transmitting on unused TV channels.

One of the ways 802.11 af reduces interference is by determines the frequency channels available for use at a given time and position. This is done by querying the internet for Geo-location database provided by a regional regulatory agency. The Geo-location database provides the frequencies being used in the specific location, and 802.11 af makes sure to not transmitting at those frequencies to limit interference from existing users.

Data Rates

802.11 af at the physical layer uses OFDM similar to 802.11 ac. The width of the frequency channels are from 6-8 MHz and can be controlled by the

---

[17] "IEEE 802.11af-2013 - IEEE Standard for Information ...." 21 Feb. 2014, https://standards.ieee.org/standard/802_11af-2013.html. Accessed 10 Oct. 2019.

regulatory authority. 802.11 af also allows for MIMO operation, and it can possibly support up to 4 streams of data. The achievable data rate per special stream is 26.7 Mbps for 6 and 7 MHz channels and 35.6 Mbps for 8 MHz channels. With four special streams and four bonded channels, the maximum data rate for AF is around 426.7 Mbps for the 6 and 7 MHz channels and 568.9 Mbps for the 8 MHz channels.

Applications

The primary benefit for 802.11 af over traditional Wi-Fi 802.11 specification is that it can work well for long range devices because it can utilize several unused TV channels at once. Potentially, this range could be up to several miles, and 802.11 af is designed to provide high data rates at these longer distances.

Constraints

The key constraint with 802.11 af is that it requires very expensive and band specific hardware. The other issue is that the White space channels are not available everywhere, especially in big cities, where most of the channels are crowded out by existing TV providers.

The related issue is that AF is not really a global standard; it is specific to U.S. and Canada, and the certification of the spectrum has to be provided on a country by country basis.

Deployment

Even though 802.11 af was released in 2014, but it never took off for several reasons. The first reason was the complexities surrounding geo-location and maintaining the geo-location database.

So, for example, if you're located in California, you might be allowed to use a certain UHF channel that is free in your area. But if you travel to a different city, let's say D.C., and try to use the same channel, it might be owned by a broadcaster that might be actively transmitting on that channel.

The other problem is that the radios for the af devices need to be specifically designed to work across the different UHF spectrum frequencies. So for any device to be effective, it would have required creating equipment that can work across all channels of the UHF spectrum, and this has proved to be prohibitively expensive.

8.4. 802.11 ah (Wi-Fi HaLow)

IEEE 802.11 ah[18] is also known as Wi-Fi HaLow. 802.11 ah defines a wireless LAN system operating at the sub one gigahertz license exempt bands. The ah protocol was approved in September 2016 and was finally published around May 2017.

The key characteristic of 802.11 ah is that it provides a favourable propagation technology because of the low frequency spectra, thereby providing an increased transmission range. The primary purpose of ah was to create extended range Wi-Fi networks that can go beyond the typical networks in the 2.4 GHz and 5 GHz space and at higher data speeds of up to 347 Mbps.

The other requirement for ah was to have lower energy consumption to make it suitable for Internet of Things applications and at the same time allow communication across longer ranges without using a lot of energy.

802.11 ah intends to be, in its power consumption profile, competitive with low power Bluetooth but at a much wider range than can be afforded by Bluetooth. Because of the low frequency, it also penetrates walls and obstructions much better, compared to the typical networks. 802.11 ah is ideal for short and bursting data that doesn't consume a good deal of power and need to travel over long distances.

Applications

The key application for ah was targeted around large scale sensor networks. Traditional applications were aimed to extend the range for public hotspots and outdoor Wi-Fi for city level traffic offloading. Applications were also targeted around smart building applications, for example, smart lighting and

---

[18] "IEEE 802.11ah-2016 - IEEE Standard for Information ...." 5 May. 2017, https://standards.ieee.org/standard/802_11ah-2016.html. Accessed 10 Oct. 2019.

smart security systems. Similarly there are application for smart cities concepts, like parking garages and parking meters.

Deployment

Even though ah, or HaLow as it is known, was released in 2016, it hasn't seen widespread adoption. The primary reason for not seeing widespread adoption is because of the lack of a global standard.

80 percent of the world currently uses 2.4 and 5 GHz Wi-Fi, which means you can connect on the typical Wi-Fi standards anywhere in the world. But a similar global standard for 900 MHz does not exist. And because of this, HaLow has been very US-centric.

The other issue has been that there are competing technologies in the market that work better to address the needs of Internet of Things (IOT). For example, Bluetooth 4 and Bluetooth 5 specifically have low energy settings that provides for IOT communication scenarios much better than what ah can do right now.

gordon.colbach@cloudversity.com

8.5. 802.11 ai

IEEE 802.11 ai[19] is an extension to the IEEE 802.11 standard and adds newer mechanisms for faster initial link setup time (FILS). 802.11 ai was published in June 2017, and allows a wireless LAN client to achieve secure link setup within 100 ms.

The primary objective of 802.11 ai is to improve operation of wireless LAN, especially the connection signaling overhead in dense environments. Fast initial link setup time, also known as FILS, enables fast roaming and addresses the key operator concerns about a poor offload experience to wireless LAN. Connection signaling overhead also slows handoff between hotspot access points.

802.11 ai also addresses a certain kind of denial of service (DOS) attacks which have plagued previous wireless LANs. These DOS attacks happen in the form of 'probe storms' where multiple devices repeatedly try to connect and disconnect from an access point and can lead to service outages.

Deployment

802.11 ai was published in June 2017, and is seeing some adoption in 2019. The Intel wireless daemon[20] (IWD) that is slated to replace the wps_supplicant in Linux added support for the fast initial link setup time in May 2019.

The wpa_supplicant runs on the client devices and controls the authentication, association and roaming of a wireless LAN driver. wpa_supplicant runs in the background as a 'daemon' program controlling the wireless connection.

---

[19] "IEEE 802.11ai-2016 - IEEE Standard for Information ...." 30 Dec. 2016, https://standards.ieee.org/standard/802_11ai-2016.html. Accessed 10 Oct. 2019.
[20] "iwd - ArchWiki." 28 Sep. 2019, https://wiki.archlinux.org/index.php/Iwd. Accessed 10 Oct. 2019.

70

8.6. 802.11 aj (China Milli-Meter Wave)

IEEE 802.11 aj[21] is a rebranding of 802.11 ad, specifically for use in the 45 GHz unlicensed spectrum available in some regions of the world. aj is specifically targeted towards China; hence, it is also known as the China Milli-Meter Wave (CMMV).

The key objective of 802.11 aj is to maintain backward compatibility with 802.11 ad which operates in the 60 GHz band. aj can operate in the 59-64 GHz range to work with ad devices and can also operate in the China 45 GHz band while maintaining a similar 802.11 user experience.

---

[21] "IEEE 802.11aj-2018 - IEEE Standard for Information Technology." 18 Apr. 2018, https://standards.ieee.org/standard/802_11aj-2018.html. Accessed 10 Oct. 2019.

8.7. 802.11 aq

IEEE 802.11 aq[22] is an amendment to the 802.11 standard that allows for pre-association discovery of services provided by the network or any device in the network.

aq extends some of the mechanisms that were initially introduced in 802.11 u[23], which enabled the discovery of devices in a network. aq extends these mechanisms to provide discovery of services running on different devices as well as those provided by the network itself.

aq was approved in June 2018 and resolves the problem of discovery of services by specifying the parameters for pre-association queries between wireless networks and devices.

At the moment, without aq, it is not possible to identify the services offered by a wireless network without connecting to it. There is also no way to determine if a wireless client device is compatible with the wireless network without actually connecting to the network.

Using aq, users can quickly identify what types of services are provided by a network and then make a decision to connect with the wireless network.

aq also has an added benefit of providing operators with an additional revenue generation opportunity as they can advertise their available services with their access points. This capability allows the operator to differentiate the service offerings from the competitors and install differentiated access points to cater to different kinds of customers.

---

[22] "IEEE 802.11aq-2018 - IEEE Approved Draft Standard for ...." 31 Aug. 2018, https://standards.ieee.org/standard/802_11aq-2018.html. Accessed 10 Oct. 2019.
[23] "IEEE 802.11u-2011 - IEEE Standard for Information ...." 25 Feb. 2011, https://standards.ieee.org/standard/802_11u-2011.html. Accessed 10 Oct. 2019.

8.8. 802.11 ay (Next Generation 60 Ghz)

IEEE 802.11 ay[24] is also known as Next-Generation 60 GHz WLAN technology. ay is still being developed, and the task group is expecting a final approval by March 2020.

The 802.11 ay amendment defines a new physical layer for WLAN networks to operate in the 60 GHz millimeter wave spectrum. The ay amendment is an extension of the existing ad specification and primarily targeted to extend throughput range and the use-cases of ad.

The final throughput potential of 802.11 ay is expected to be around 20 Gbps as per the specification. The primary use-cases for ay include indoor operation, out-door back-haul connection amongst different wireless networks and short-range communications.

The peak transmission rate of AY is expected to be 20 Gbps and the primary extensions to the underlying WLAN specification include channel bonding of 2, 3, and 4 channels, MIMO, and higher modulation schemes.

---

[24] "802.11 ay - IEEE 802." http://www.ieee802.org/11/Reports/tgay_update.htm. Accessed 10 Oct. 2019.

8.9. 802.11 be (Extremely High Throughput)

IEEE 802.11 be[25], also known as extremely high throughput amendment, is the next potential amendment for the 802.11 standard.

be will probably build upon the 802.11 ax standard and focuses on wireless LAN indoor and outdoor operations for stationary and pedestrian use-cases in the 2.4, 5, and 6 GHz frequency bands.

802.11 be is the most likely successor of ax; hence the Wi-Fi Alliance will most likely certify it as Wi-Fi 7. 802.11 ax is the current latest standard of Wi-Fi and is classified as Wi-Fi 6 by the Wi-Fi Alliance.

---

[25] "[1902.04320] IEEE 802.11be Extremely High Throughput: The ...." 12 Feb. 2019, https://arxiv.org/abs/1902.04320. Accessed 10 Oct. 2019.

8.10. 802.11 az (Next-Generation Positioning)

IEEE 802.11 az[26] focuses on Next-Generation Positioning Technology. 802.11 az can be considered a successor of 802.11mc, which was added to the core 802.11 specification around 2016.

az improves on the absolute and relative location tracking and positioning of client devices using Fine Timing Measurement (FTM). FTM is based on the round-trip time of a transmitted signal from the client device to the access point. Techniques in use today to measure distance to the access point utilise signal-strength estimations and are supposed to be in order of magnitude less accurate than the round-trip time measurements.

Although the round-trip time measurement was introduced in 802.11 mc, 802.11 az also specifies modifications to the MAC and physical layers to reduce existing wireless medium use and power consumption primarily aimed to help scale positioning in dense deployments.

The final 802.11 az standard is expected to be published by 2021.

---

[26] "IEEE P802.11 - NEXT GENERATION POSITIONING STUDY ...."
http://www.ieee802.org/11/Reports/tgaz_update.htm. Accessed 10 Oct. 2019.

8.11. 802.11 ba (Wake-up Radio)

IEEE 802.11 ba[27] specifies a wake-up radio (WUR) format to develop an additional radio separate from that used for data transmission.

The new smaller radio is used to turn on the primary radio as required with a very low latency, thus improving the power efficiency of the overall system. The key benefit of 802.11 ba is to extend the battery life of devices and sensors, targeted primarily to an Internet of Things setting.

Exact timelines for 802.11 ba are not currently available, and hopefully the standard should be up by July 2020.

----

[27] "802.11ba Battery Life Improvement - Preview: IEEE ...." 1 Nov. 2017, https://ieeexplore.ieee.org/document/8053470/versions. Accessed 10 Oct. 2019.

8.12. 802.11 bb (Li-Fi)

IEEE 802.11 bb[28] is also known as Li-Fi. 802.11 bb is the first 802.11 standard that targets short-range indoor communication using visible light.

802.11 bb standard operates in the 380 nm to 5000 nm band, and the goal is to achieve minimum single link throughput of around 10 Mbps. It also specifies at least one mode of operation that achieves a single-link throughput of at least 5 Gbps.

802.11 bb is still under planning, and no schedule is available for publication or acceptance into the standard.

---

[28] "ieee p802.11 - light communication task group - IEEE 802." http://www.ieee802.org/11/Reports/tgbb_update.htm. Accessed 10 Oct. 2019.

8.13. 802.11 bc (Enhanced broadcast services)

IEEE 802.11 bc[29] provides for enhanced broadcast services to the 802.11 specification. 802.11 bc enables broadcasting of authenticated data to both associated and unassociated client devices.

The goal is not only to enable broadcast from access points, but also to enable stations and client devices to broadcast to everybody else in the network. No task group schedule is currently available for bc, and it remains a work in progress.

---

[29] "[802SEC] IEEE 802.11bc and IEEE 802.11bd draft PAR and ...." 18 Sep. 2018, http://grouper.ieee.org/groups///802/secmail/msg22778.html. Accessed 10 Oct. 2019.

8.14. 802.11 bd (Next-Generation Vehicular)

IEEE 802.11 bd[30] provides the Next-Generation Vehicular or NGV technology to the underlying 802.11 wireless LAN networks.

The first specification for communication in vehicular environments was done by 802.11 p[31]. The 802.11 p standard specifies protocols for using Wi-Fi in stationary and moving vehicle environments and communicating with other vehicles and roadside infrastructure. The 802.11 p specification provides for Wi-Fi-based communication even at speeds above 200 km an hour.

802.11 p, also known as V2X, specifies the use of 10 MHz of spectrum in the 5.9 GHz band via unassociated communications. Unassociated communication means there is no need to authenticate between different vehicles. This ensures that the overhead is low thereby resulting in a fast setup time to enable quick communications.

The 802.11 bb standard is designed to enhance the throughput and the range and take advantage of the latest 802.11 technologies since 802.11p and merge them into the 802.11 specification. This also will allow for use of the 6 GHz unlicensed bands in the final bd specification.

802.11 bd is planned for the future, and there is no timeline available right now. The task group though has started to work on bd - the specification being a couple of years in the future.

---

[30] "IEEE 802.11bd & 5G NR V2X: Evolution of Radio ... - arXiv." 26 Mar. 2019, https://arxiv.org/pdf/1903.08391. Accessed 10 Oct. 2019.
[31] "IEEE 802.11p-2010 - IEEE Standard for Information ...." 15 Jul. 2010, https://standards.ieee.org/standard/802_11p-2010.html. Accessed 10 Oct. 2019.

9. ALTERNATE TECHNOLOGIES TO 802.11

9.1. HiperLAN 2

HiperLAN 2 is a wireless LAN technology operating in the license free 5 GHz (5.4 to 5.7 GHz) U-NII band. Under development by the European Telecommunications Standardization Institute (ETSI) Broadband Radio Access Networks (BRAN) project, HiperLAN 2 is designed to carry ATM cells, IP packets, firewire packets, and digital data from cellular phones. Whereas 802.11a is a form of wireless Ethernet, HiperLAN 2 is commonly regarded as wireless ATM.

An extension of the 802.11 standard, 802.11a is connectionless Ethernet-like standard, meaning there isn't a persistent connection between client and server. On the other hand, HiperLAN 2 is based on connection-oriented links, though it can accept Ethernet frames. 802.11a is optimized for data communications, as are all standards based on 802.11.

HiperLAN 2 is best suited to wireless multimedia because of its integrated Quality of Service (QoS) support. HiperLAN 2 will have a difficult time competing with the momentum of 802.11a for several reasons. 802.11a has year head start over HiperLAN 2. In addition, the 802.11 group looking for ways to incorporate the best features of HiperLAN 2 within its own standards.

9.2. HomeRF

HomeRF was the first practical wireless home networking technology and came out in mid-2000 [32]. HomeRF stands for Home Radio Frequency, as it uses radio frequencies to transmit data over ranges of 75 to 125 feet.

HomeRF uses SWAP (Shared Wireless Access Protocol), which is a hybrid standard, developed from IEEE 802.11. SWAP can connect up to 127 network devices and transmits at speeds up to 2Mbps. Overall the major disadvantage to a HomeRF network is data transmission speed.

Two Mbps is fine for sharing files and printing normal files. It is insufficient for streaming media and printing or transferring large graphic files. HomeRF still provides some advantages to those wanting a less expensive wired network solution. HomeRF also does not interfere with Bluetooth and is better for transmitting voice signals.

---

[32] "HomeRF FREQUENTLY ASKED QUESTIONS."
http://www.cazitech.com/HomeRF%20FAQ%20-%20USA.PDF. Accessed 7 Nov. 2017.

10. WiMax

There is a good chance that the words that you are reading now are coming over a broadband connection, like a DSL/cable Internet service. However, if you were in a remote farm in New Zealand, searching the Web for the right fertilizer to raise your crops, you might be using a dial-up connection over a noisy telephone line. But with WiMax, which is capable of transmitting large amounts of data over long distances, you could be surfing the web looking for the appropriate fertilizer, over a 75 Mbps connection without a wire!

In major metropolitan areas in the United States and many other countries, broadband access has been dominated by wired technologies such as DSL/cable, which use existing infrastructure such as telephone lines/television cable network to provide high speed Internet access. WLAN/WiFi® is another term often associated with high speed Internet though it is limited to local area networks (LAN).

Whereas DSL/cable technologies operate at WAN/MAN (metropolitan area network) ranges. WiFi is designed to work with DSL/cable to share the Internet connection between several computers in a local home/office network. DSL/cable technologies require telephone/cable lines to be laid over long distances to serve customers.

In countries such as India, Mexico or Brazil, the potential for broadband access is extremely high, taking into account the trend of Internet requirements. However, the penetration of DSL/cable is not as high, mainly due to a lack of reliable infrastructure, cables or backbone switching equipment.

A viable complement to DSL/cable based service is WiMax or wireless broadband, which connects users to the Internet, even in places where the infrastructure might not be as developed. At first glance, WiMax would seem similar to 3G cellular technologies, since both these networks can transmit data and voice, but by design, cellular 3G is voice-centric while WiMax is data-centric.

WiMax can achieve data rates up to 75Mbps and a theoretical 30 mile reach, however, in typical deployment scenarios, data rates fall with increasing reach. Geographically WiMax is flexible and can improve yield due to wiring/labor cost savings. It is very likely that service providers will use the tiered pricing approach and service contracts that they currently employ for DSL/cable.

WiMax (Worldwide Interoperability for Microwave Access) is a wireless broadband technology, which supports point to multipoint (PMP) broadband wireless access.

WiMax is basically a new shorthand term for IEEE Standard 802.16, which was designed to support the European standards. 802.16's predecessors (like 802.11a) were not very accommodative of the European standards, per se.

The IEEE wireless standard has a range of up to 30 miles, and can deliver broadband at around 75 megabits per second. This is theoretically, 20 times faster than a commercially available wireless broadband.

The 802.16 WiMax standard was published in March 2002 and provided updated information on the Metropolitan Area Network (MAN) technology. The extension given in the March publication, extended the line-of-sight fixed wireless MAN standard, focused solely on a spectrum from 10 GHz to 60+ GHz.

This extension provides for non-line of sight access in low frequency bands like 2 - 11 GHz. These bands are sometimes unlicensed. This also boosts the maximum distance from 31 to 50 miles and supports PMP (point to multipoint) and mesh technologies. The IEEE approved the 802.16 standards in June 2004, and three working groups were formed to evaluate and rate the standards.

WiMax can be used for wireless networking like the popular WiFi. WiMax, a second-generation protocol, allows higher data rates over longer distances, efficient use of bandwidth, and avoids interference almost to a minimum. WiMax can be termed partially a successor to the Wi-Fi protocol, which is measured in feet, and works over shorter distances.

11. WiMax Concept

Fixed wireless is the base concept for the metropolitan area networking (MAN), given in the 802.16 standard. In fixed wireless, a backbone of base stations is connected to a public network.

Each of these base stations supports many fixed subscriber stations, either public WiFi hotspots or firewalled enterprise networks. These base stations use the media access control (MAC) layer, and allocate uplink and downlink bandwidth to subscribers as per their individual needs. This is basically on a real-time need basis.

The subscriber stations might also be mounted on rooftops of the users. The MAC layer is a common interface that makes the networks interoperable. In the future, one can look forward to 802.11 hotspots, hosted by 802.16 MANs. These would serve as wireless local area networks (LANs) and would serve the end users directly too.

WiMax supporters are focusing on the broadband last mile in unwired areas, and on backhaul for WiFi hotspots. WiMax is expected to support mobile wireless technology too, wireless transmissions directly to mobile end users.

WiMax changes the last mile problem for broadband in the same way as WiFi has changed the last one hundred feet of networking.

WiMAX has a range of up to 31 miles, which can be used to provide both campus-level network connectivity and a wireless last-mile approach that can bring high-speed networking and Internet service directly to customers. This is especially useful in those areas that were not served by cable or DSL or in areas where the local telephone company may need a long time to deploy broadband service.

12. WiMax Forum

WiMax, like DSL/cable is standards based and enables vendors to interoperate with one another. The IEEE standard 802.16 was specified for Worldwide Interoperability for Microwave Access (WiMax). This standard has been further revised for 2-11GHz fixed (802.16.a-2004) and 2-6GHz portable (802.16e) wireless solutions.

The WiMax Forum[33] has been chartered with taking the standards (IEEE/ETSI) and implementing interoperable solutions for WiMax. The forum is comprised of a group of diverse companies, ranging from silicon vendors to equipment manufacturers to wireless carriers, all having a stake in the deployment of WiMax.

The WiMax Forum conducts a number of interoperability events, to bring vendors on common ground. There will also be a WiMax certification for interoperability with multiple vendors, similar to the TR-067 Interoperability tests for DSL or WiFi certification.

WiMax Forum was formed in April 2001 to promote conformance and interoperability of the standard IEEE 802.16. The Forum's founding

_____

[33] "WiMAX Forum." http://wimaxforum.org/. Accessed 17 Jan. 2018.

members were Ensemble, CrossSpan, Harris and Nokia.

In April 2002, the forum grew to accommodate another member OFDM, and in November, added Fujitsu as its sixth member. In March 2003, after intensive lobbying for the just cause of promoting the standard by Fujitsu and Wi-LAN, many new members joined the WiMax forum.

The forum was formed solely for promotion of devices supported by the 802.16 standard. The forum takes responsibility also to develop devices conforming to the standard and releasing it in the market. Some prominent members of the WiMax Forum are Airspan, Alvarion, Analog Devices, Aperto Networks, Ensemble Communications, Fujitsu, Intel, Nokia, OFDM Forum, Proxim and Wi-LAN.

The new members were Aperto, Alvarion, Airspan, Intel, Proxim and others. The current forum has strong presence from service providers, system manufacturers, chip vendors and eco-system vendors. Currently the WiMax forum has 110 members.

Typical WiMax equipment would contain a baseband-PHY processor and the MAC network processor besides memory and other peripherals. WiMax uses Orthogonal Frequency Division Multiplexing (OFDM) for modulation in its physical layer, which bundles data over narrowband carriers transmitted in parallel at different frequencies.

The same technique has been used as Discrete Multi-tone Modulation (DMT) in ADSL. OFDM makes WiMax scalable for a fluctuating user base, since the spectrum can be dynamically re-allocated (range: 1.25-20 MHz) with variations in the number of subscribers. In addition, OFDM improves resilience to interference and outdoor environment, and improves the signal to noise ratio at the terminals.

There are a number of challenges facing WiMax including:

- RF interference and attenuation
- Operator contention for infrastructure placement to maximize performance and reach
- Government regulations, spectral licensing/usage management
- Concerns with WiMax base station market growth due to bias towards voice networks

13. WiMax Protocol

WiMax has two main topologies namely Point-to-Point for backhaul and Point-to-Multipoint Base station for Subscriber station.

In each of these situations, multiple input multiple output antennas are used. The protocol structure of IEEE 802.16 Broadband wireless MAN standard is shown below:

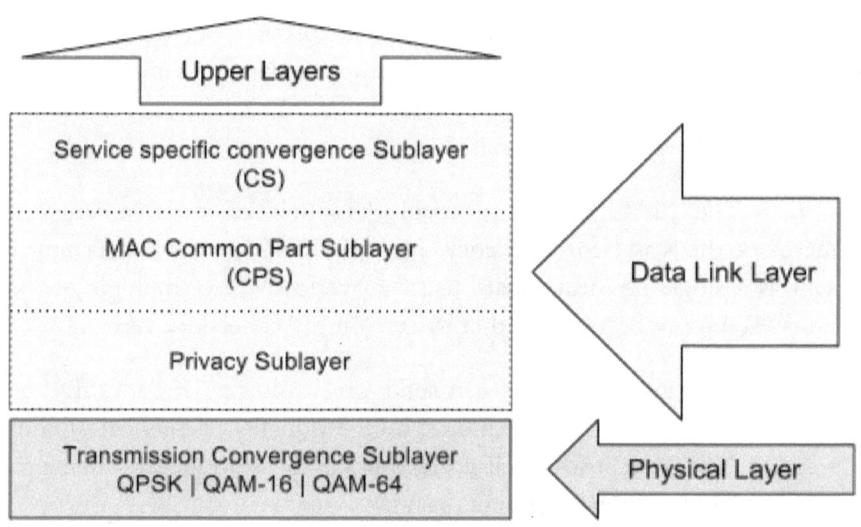

Figure 11: Protocol Structure of IEEE 802.16

The above picture shows four layers: Convergence, MAC, Transmission and Physical. These layers map to two of the lowest layers: physical and data link layers of the OSI model.

WiMax provides many user applications and interfaces like Ethernet, TDM, ATM, IP, and VLAN.

The IEEE 802.16 standard is versatile enough to accommodate time division multiplexing (TDM) or frequency division duplexing (FDD) deployments and also allows for both full and half-duplex terminals.

802.16 supports three physical layers. The mandatory physical mode is 256-point FFT OFDM (Orthogonal Frequency Division Multiplexing). The other modes are Single carrier (SC) and 2048 OFDMA (Orthogonal Frequency Division Multiplexing Access) modes. The corresponding European standard - the ETSI Hiperman standard defines a single PHY mode identical to the 256 OFDM modes in the 802.16d standard.

The MAC was developed for a point-to-multipoint wireless access environment and can accommodate protocols like ATM, Ethernet and IP (Internet Protocol). The MAC frame structure dynamic uplink and downlink profiles of terminals as per the link conditions. This is to ensure a trade-off of capacity and real-time robustness.

The MAC uses a protocol data unit of variable length, which increases the standards efficiency. Multiple MAC protocol data unit can be sent as a single physical stream to save overload. Also, multiple Service data units (SDU) can be sent together to save on MAC header overhead.

By fragmenting, you can send large volumes of data (SDUs) across frame boundaries and can guarantee a QoS (Quality of Service) of competing services. The MAC uses a self-correcting bandwidth request scheme to avoid overhead and acknowledgement delays.

This also allows better QoS handling than the traditional acknowledged schemes. The terminals have a variety of options to request for bandwidth depending on the QoS and other parameters. The signal requirement can be polled or a request can be piggybacked.

The 802.16 MAC protocol performs mainly two tasks: Periodic and Aperiodic activities. Fast activities (periodic) like scheduling, packing, fragmentation and ARQ are hard-pressed for time and have hard tight deadlines. They must be performed within a single frame.

The slow activities, on the other hand, typically execute as per pre-fixed timers, but are not associated with any timers. They also do not have a specific time frame or deadline.

14. WiMax Architecture

WiMax offers a rich feature set and flexibility, which also increases the complexity of service deployment and provisioning for fixed and mobile networks.

Let us take a look at the WiMax Management Information Base (MIB).

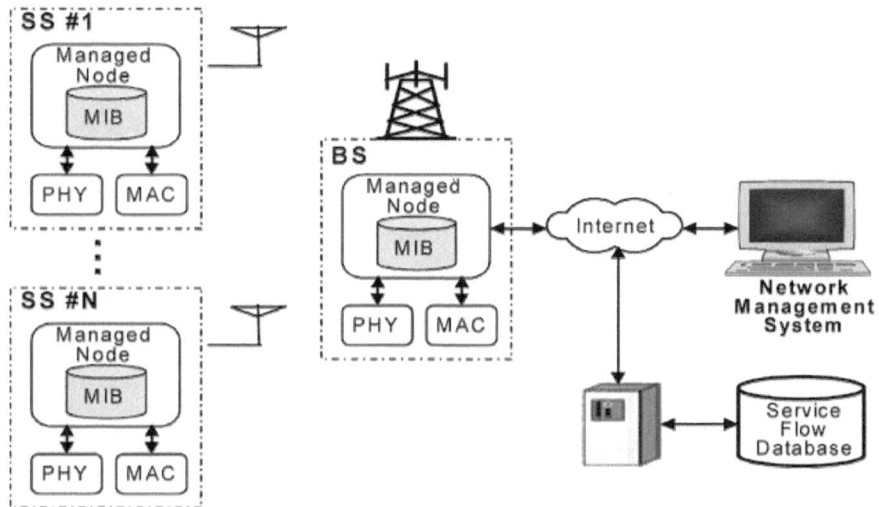

Figure 12: WiMax Management Information Base

The above figure shows the management reference model for BWA (Broadband Wireless Access) networks. This consists of a Network Management System (NMS), some nodes, and a database.

BS and SS managed nodes collect and store the managed objects in an 802.16 MIB format. Managed objects are made available to NMS' using the Simple Network Management Protocol (SNMP).

When a customer subscribes to the WiMax service, the service provider asks the customer for the service flow information. This would include number of UL/DL connections with the data rates and QoS parameters. The customer also needs to tell the kind of applications that he proposes to run.

The service provider then proceeds to pre-provision the services and enters the information in the Service Flow Database.

15. WiMax Competing Technologies

As we learnt in the previous pages, that WiMax was formed to complement Bluetooth and WiFi technologies, let us look at the differences in each of these:

Table 4: Difference between WiMax, WLAN and Bluetooth

	WiMax	**WLAN**	**Bluetooth**
Frequency	2 - 11 GHz	2.4 GHz	Varies
Range	~50,000 meters	~100 meters	~10 meters
Data Transfer Rate	70 mbps	11 - 55 mbps	20 - 55 mbps
Users	1000s	< 100	~ 10

The 802.11 is based on a distributed architecture, whereas, WiMax is based on a centrally controlled architecture. In this the scheduler residing in the Base Station (BS) has the complete control of the wireless media access.

WiMax can support multiple connections conforming to a set of QoS parameters and provides the packet classifier ability to map the connections to many user applications and interfaces.

WiFi and WiMax may end up complementing each other, but a new technology, IEEE 802.20, might give them both a run for their money. IEEE 802.20 standard like the 802.16 is aimed at wireless high-speed connectivity to mobile consumer devices like cellular phones, PDAs and laptops. It will operate in the 500 MHz - 3.5 GHz and is led by Flarion Technologies and ArrayComm.

16. CONCLUSION

Bluetooth and WiFi have the potential to dramatically alter how people use devices to connect and communicate in everyday life. Bluetooth is a low-power, short-range technology for ad hoc cable replacement; it enables people to wirelessly combine devices wherever they bring them.

Conversely, WiFi is a moderate-range, moderate-speed technology based on Ethernet; it allows people to wirelessly access an organizational network throughout a campus location. Although the technologies share the 2.4 GHz band, have potentially overlapping applications, and have been pitted against each other in the press, they do not compete and can even be successfully combined for corporate use.

One thing is clear, wireless technologies will continue to evolve and offer organizations and end users higher standard of life by making us more mobile and increasing our ability to interact with each other, removing distance as a barrier.

Wireless technologies have already enabled travelers to sit in any airport or hotel and surf the Web or connect to the home office and work. Users can now surf or work in places such as malls, parks, or (with smaller handheld computers) just walking down the street.

Internet service providers are installing larger wireless networks allowing users to connect from anywhere in the city. The rapid progression of wireless technologies have resulted in a scenario where the network follows you instead of you following the network in just a span of a decade.